SPAIN

Cath Senker

Photographs by Sue Cunningham

CHERRYTREE BOOKS

Distributed in the United States by
Cherrytree Books
1980 Lookout Drive
North Mankato, MN 56001

Library of Congress Cataloging-in-Publication Data
Senker, Cath.
   Spain / Cath Senker.
      p.cm. -- (Letters from around the world)
   Includes index.
   ISBN 1-84234-249-5 (alk. paper)
   13-digit ISBN (from 1 January 2007) 978-1-84234-249-7
   1. Spain--Social life and customs--Juvenile literature. 2.
Spain--Description and travel--Juvenile literature. 3.
Children--Spain--Correspondence--Juvenile literature. I.
Title. II. Series.

DP48.S435 2004
946.083--dc22

                         2004041447

First Edition
9 8 7 6 5 4 3 2 1

First published by
Evans Brothers Ltd
2A Portman Mansions
Chiltern Street
London W1U 6NR

Conceived and produced by

Nutshell
MEDIA

www.nutshellmedialtd.co.uk

Editor: Polly Goodman
Design: Mayer Media Ltd
Cartography: Encompass Graphics Ltd
Artwork: Mayer Media Ltd
Consultants: Jeff Stanfield and Anne Spiring

© Copyright Evans Brothers Limited 2003

All photographs were taken by Sue Cunningham.

Printed in China.

Acknowledgments
The author and photographer would like to thank the
following for their help with this book: the Pizarro Sos
family — Juan, Vivi, Juan, Julia, and Claudia; Carmina Sos;
Clare Applewhite; the principal, staff, and students of José
María del Campo School, Seville.

Cover: Julia and her friends by the river.
Title page: Julia and her sister play a clapping game.
This page: A view of the river Guadalquivir.
Contents page: Julia wearing her flamenco dress.
Glossary page: Julia points to Andalusia on the map.
Further information page: Julia's home-made *gazpacho*.
Index: Julia and her family on their way to the park.

Contents

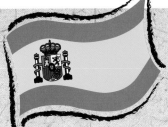

My Country

Friday, January 4

Calle Luz Arriero 20
Apartment 1A
Seville
14361
Spain

Dear Kim,

Hola! (This means "hello" in Spanish.)

My name's Julia (you say "Hoo-lia") Pizarro Sos and I'm 7 years old. I live in Seville, in southern Spain. I have an older brother named Juan — he's 10. My little sister, Claudia, is 5.

I hope you can help me with my English. I learn English at an after-school club.

Write back soon!

From
Julia

Here's my family, from the front: Claudia, me, Juan, Mom, and Dad.

Spain is divided into many regions. Seville is in a region called Andalusia. The Canary Islands also belong to Spain. They are in the Atlantic Ocean, off the north coast of Africa.

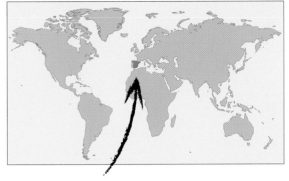

Spain's place in the world.

N

FRANCE

ANDORRA

PYRENEES

Duero

Zaragoza

Barcelona

SPAIN

ATLANTIC OCEAN

MADRID

Majorca

PORTUGAL

Tagus

Valencia

Ibiza

SIERRA MORENA

Mediterranean Sea

Guadalquivir

Seville

ANDALUSIA

SIERRA NEVADA

Mulhacen
11,408 ft
(3,478 m)

Canary Islands

La Palma

Lanzarote

Tenerife

Fuerteventura

Gran Canaria

Malaga

ATLANTIC OCEAN

0   100 kilometers
0   100 miles

Tarifa

0   50   100   150   200 kilometers

0   50   100 miles

ALGERIA

MOROCCO

Spain is in southern Europe, between the Mediterranean Sea and the Atlantic Ocean.

5

This photo of Seville was taken from the top of the city's cathedral tower.

Seville is an exciting city. It has changed a lot over the last few years. In 1992 there was a big international exhibition. New buildings were built specially, and a fast train service to Madrid started up.

Seville has the only river port in Spain. It is important for trade. Farm goods leave the country by boat, and cars and machinery are brought in.

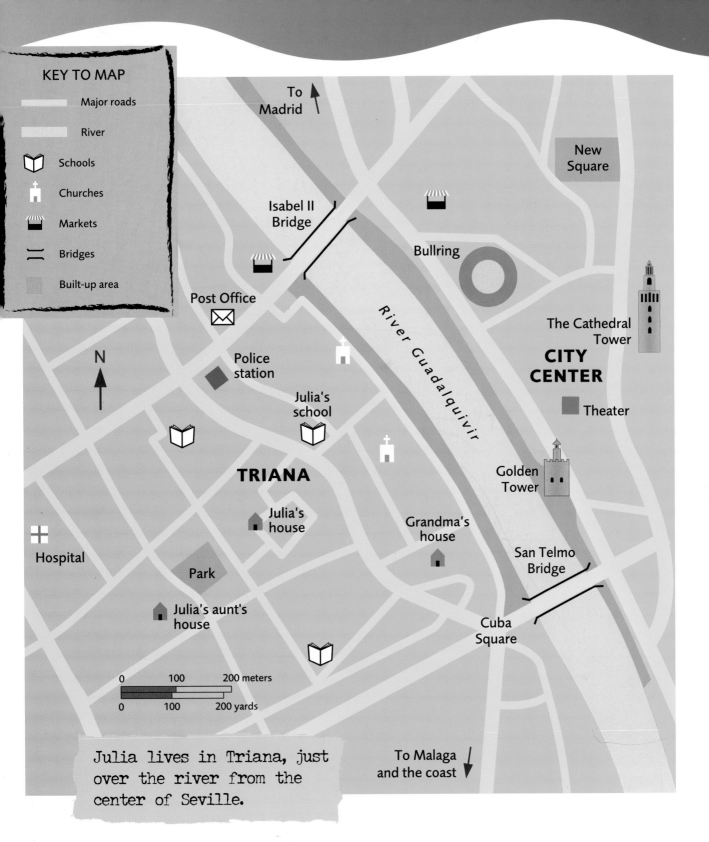

To Madrid ↑

New Square

Isabel II Bridge

Bullring

River Guadalquivir

Post Office ✉

N ↑

Police station

Julia's school

The Cathedral Tower

CITY CENTER

Theater

TRIANA

Golden Tower

Julia's house

Grandma's house

Park

San Telmo Bridge

Hospital

Julia's aunt's house

Cuba Square

0	100	200 meters
0	100	200 yards

To Malaga and the coast ↓

Julia lives in Triana, just over the river from the center of Seville.

Many tourists visit Seville. They come to see the beautiful old buildings and watch flamenco dancing. There is bullfighting, too.

Landscape and Weather

Seville is in a very flat area. To the north of the city is a range of hills. To the west is the coast, about an hour's drive away by car.

The River Guadalquivir runs through the center of Seville.

Seville is hotter than most parts of Spain. In the summer it is baking hot, dry, and dusty. Even in winter, the temperature rarely falls below freezing. There are just a few very chilly days. Usually there is only a little rain. When it does rain in spring and autumn, it pours!

Seville's Climate

January

Temperature
59 °F
(15 °C)

Rainfall
0–1 in
(19 mm)

July

Temperature
97 °F
(36 °C)

Rainfall
0 in
(0 mm)

There are lots of olive groves around Seville. The hot climate is perfect for growing olives and oranges.

At Home

Like many people in Seville, Julia's family lives in an apartment. It is on the second floor of a building. The building has a courtyard. Everyone in the building shares the courtyard. They all dry their washing on the building's flat roof.

Julia and Claudia ring the buzzer at the entrance to their apartment building.

Washing dries quickly on the flat roof of Julia's apartment building.

These are recycling barrels. The green one is for glass. The blue one is for paper. "*Vidrio*" is Spanish for "glass." "*Papel*" means "paper."

The garbage cans of the apartments are out on the street. There are also barrels for recycling paper, cardboard, glass, and plastic.

Each apartment has a mailbox in the hallway by the front door.

Julia and Claudia have
bunk beds. Julia sleeps
in the top one.

Julia's flat has three bedrooms,
a living room, a kitchen, and two
bathrooms. There are shutters
outside all the windows to keep
out the heat in summer.

Julia and Claudia share a
bedroom. Their brother Juan
has his own room.

Julia enjoys coloring.
She also does her
homework at this desk.

Saturday, February 9

Calle Luz Arriero 20
Apartment 1A
Seville
14361
Spain

Hola Kim!

Thanks for your letter. I don't like the rain either. It's been quite cold here for the last few days. We don't have central heating or carpets because it's usually so hot. When it's chilly, we use a special table, the *mesa de camilla* (you say "cam-eeya") in the living room. It has a heater underneath and a cover to keep in the heat. The *mesa de camilla* makes the room cozy.

Keep warm!

Love

Julia

This is my family in our living room. The *mesa de camilla* is in the center.

Food and Mealtimes

Julia has breakfast at 8:30 A.M. Spanish people often eat toast and jam for breakfast. In the south they also like toast with olive oil.

Children often prefer cereal and milk for breakfast.

Julia has lunch at 2:30 P.M. It is the main meal. Her favorite dish is *paella*. She also likes rice with chicken, or potatoes and fish.

Julia helps her grandma make *paella*. It is made from rice, seafood, and vegetables.

The children often eat first. Then the adults enjoy a quiet lunch afterward.

Everyone has a sandwich or some cookies at about 6 P.M. to keep them going until supper at 9 P.M. Supper is usually a light meal of eggs, fish, or meat with salad.

Julia, Juan, Claudia, and their mom buy fresh fruit and vegetables every day.

Julia's mom goes to the local stores to buy fresh fruit, vegetables, and bread. She buys fish at the fish shop and meat at the butcher's. She buys everything else from the supermarket.

Julia's family loves going out to eat when the weather is good.

Saturday, June 1

Calle Luz Arriero 20

Apartment 1A

Seville

14361

Spain

Hi Kim!

Here's the Spanish recipe you asked for. It's for *gazpacho* soup. It has to be eaten cold. We eat it in the summer. This is our family recipe — it's delicious!

You will need: 2 pounds fresh tomatoes, $\frac{1}{2}$ large onion, $\frac{1}{2}$ green pepper, 1 cucumber, 1 clove garlic, a little cold water, 5 tablespoons of olive oil, 3 teaspoons of white wine vinegar, salt.

1. Chop the vegetables and put them in a food processor.
2. Add the water, oil, vinegar, and a pinch of salt.
3. Mix everything up.
4. Chill in the refrigerator for 2 hours before serving.

Let me know what you think!

From

Julia

I helped Mom make this *gazpacho*.

School Day

Julia's school is very close to her home. It only takes a few minutes to walk there. It is a big school for boys and girls. Julia will go there until she is 11. There is no school uniform.

School starts at 9 A.M. and finishes at 2 P.M. There is a break at 11:30 A.M. All the children go home for lunch.

Julia always uses the pedestrian crossing on her way to school.

Julia's favorite playground game is jumping rope.

In Seville, the school summer vacation is nearly three months long. It is too hot to study in the summer.

There are 25 children in Julia's class. This is a math lesson.

Julia learns about Andalusia in a geography lesson.

In Spain, children go to nursery or preschool at the age of 4. When they are 6 years old they start primary school.

Julia's class learns Spanish, math, science, geography, music, history, and French.

This is Julia's class singing in the school theater.

Friday, October 4

Calle Luz Arriero 20
Apartment 1A
Seville
14361
Spain

Hola Kim!

Do you like school? I love it because most of my friends are there. My favorite subject is writing, but I also like doing gym. I'm quite good at sport, especially swimming and in-line skating. I have extra lessons after school. These are my after-school classes:

Tuesday
5–6 P.M. English
6–7 P.M. Karate

Thursday
5–6 P.M. English
7–8:30 P.M. In-line skating

What do you do after school?

Love

Julia

The after-school karate club is lots of fun!

Work

Julia's dad works for the government. He works with farmers and the fishing industry. He travels to his office on a motorcycle. He usually finishes work at 3 P.M.

Julia's mom works at home looking after the family. Some of her friends go out to work, mostly just in the mornings.

Here is Julia's dad in his office.

22

There are many small workshops in Seville. This man makes traditional Spanish guitars.

This man is a waiter. Seville is full of busy cafés.

Other people in Seville work in industry, or in farming outside the city. Oranges from Seville are picked to make marmalade.

Seville is popular with tourists, so many people work in hotels and cafés.

Free Time

On weekends, Julia likes in-line skating and going to the park. Sometimes the whole family goes to the countryside.

Julia's family goes on an outing to the park.

Julia's family has a small apartment near the coast, in Tarifa. They go there for weekends or short stays.

The most popular sport in Spain is soccer. Many people support their local team and watch the game each weekend.

Julia and Claudia go in-line skating in a square near their home.

Julia and Claudia play a clapping game.

Religion and Festivals

At Christmas, Julia's family has a beautiful Nativity scene at home.

Most people in Spain are Roman Catholics. There are some Protestants, Muslims, and Jews, too.

The parade at the Three Kings festival. Everyone goes wild catching candies!

Many Spanish people today are not religious, but everyone loves Christmas. The festival of the Three Kings on January 6 is the most important day of the Christmas celebrations.

Wednesday, January 8

Calle Luz Arriero 20
Apartment 1A
Seville
14361
Spain

Hi Kim!

Yesterday was so exciting! It was the festival of the Three Kings. We had a big parade through the streets. Three men dressed up as the Three Kings. There were other people in costume riding on huge floats. They threw *caramelos* (candies) to the crowds.

You would have loved it!

Do you celebrate any special festivals?

Love

Julia

Mom bought a special festival cake, called *Rosco de Reyes*. There was a little toy king hidden inside.

Fact File

Capital City: Madrid is the capital of Spain. It is right in the middle of the country.

Other Major Cities: Barcelona, Valencia, Zaragoza, Malaga, and Seville.

Neighboring Countries: France, Andorra, Portugal, and Morocco.

Size: 194,039 square miles (504,783km^2).

Population: 39.8 million.

Flag: The official Spanish flag used by the government has red and yellow stripes and a coat of arms. Sometimes the flag is shown without the coat of arms.

Languages: Spanish is the main language. There are several other languages that are spoken in different regions. The main ones are Catalan, Galician, and Basque.

Currency: The euro (€). This replaced the Spanish peseta in January 2002. There are 100 cents to the euro. Spanish stamps often show the king's head or other national symbol.

Highest Mountain: Cerro de Mulhacen 11,408 feet (3,478m) in the Sierra Nevada mountains.

Longest River: The River Tagus flows 624 miles through the middle of Spain, from east to west.

Main Industries: Spain's main industries make cars, steel, textiles, chemicals, and ships. Farming, fishing, and tourism are also important. Each year there are more than 50 million visitors to Spain.

Spanish Food: Spain is famous for *paella*, *tortilla* (a thick potato omelet), and *tapas*. A *tapa* is a small plate of food, eaten as a snack. There are hundreds of different kinds of *tapas*.

Famous Spaniards: Pablo Picasso, who was born in 1881, became one of Spain's most famous artists. Joaquín Rodrigo, born in 1901, was a great composer. He wrote beautiful music for the Spanish guitar. Paco de Lucía is the most famous flamenco guitar player. His music is known all over the world.

Main Religions: Most Spanish people are Roman Catholics. There are also Protestants, Muslims, and some Jews. Christmas and Easter are the main Catholic holidays. The main Christmas celebration is on January 6. There is a big procession, with carnival floats. People on the floats throw candies into the crowd.

Glossary

Andalusia (spelt *Andalucía* in Spanish) One of the regions of Spain. Each region is divided into smaller parts, called provinces. The city of Seville and the area around it form Seville province.

bullfighting A fight between a person and a bull. At the end, the bull is killed. Many Spanish people do not like this sport, but it is still popular.

caramelos (Say it as it looks) The Spanish word for candies.

flamenco A style of music and dance from Andalusia. There is usually a singer, a guitar player, and a dancer.

floats Large trucks carrying people dressed in festival costumes.

gazpacho (You say "gas-pacho") A cold soup made with tomatoes.

hola (You say "olla") The Spanish word for "hello."

mesa de camilla (You say "mesa d' cam-eeya") A table with a platform underneath, with a hole to place a heater in. A table cover goes over the table.

Nativity scene A model of baby Jesus and the place where he was born.

paella (You say "pie-ay-ya") A rice dish with vegetables and chicken or seafood. It is cooked and served in a large pan.

parade A special event, with people marching through the streets and music.

Rosco de Reyes A ring-shaped cake filled with cream. It is eaten at the Three Kings festival.

Three Kings festival The Roman Catholic Christmas celebration on January 6. People remember the coming of the Three Kings to visit the baby Jesus, just after he was born.

Further Information

Information Books:

Blomquist, Christopher. *A Primary Source Guide to Spain*. New York: Power Kids Press, 2005.

McKay, Susan. *Festivals of the World: Spain*. Milwaukee, WI: Gareth Stevens Publishing, 1999.

Parker, Ed. *Changing Face of Spain*. Chicago: Raintree, 2003.

Fiction:

Myers, Walter Dean. *Three Swords for Granada*. New York: Holiday House, 2002.

Segovia, Gertrudis. *The Spanish Fairy Book*. New York: Dover Publications, 2000.

Resource Pack:

Project School – resource pack about Spain, available free from:
Tourist Office of Spain, Water Tower, Place, Suite 915, East 845, North Michigan Avenue, Chicago, IL 60611

Tel. 312 / 6421992 - 9440216
Fax. 312 / 642 9817

Web sites:

CyberSpain
www.cyberspain.com
All about Spanish culture, traditions, and landscapes.

Travel for Kids
www.travelforkids.com/Funtodo/Spain/spain.htm
Details of what to see when visiting Spain.

Index